# AIN'T NATURE GRAND!

by

## Les Blacklock

VOYAGEUR PRESS

1980

For my son, Craig

First published in 1980 by Voyageur Press
  9337 Nesbitt Road, Bloomington, MN. 55437

ISBN No. 0-89658-009-1

Editor: Raymond Bechtle

Separations by Mueller Color Plate, Minneapolis, MN.

Printed by North Central Publishing Company
  St. Paul, MN.

# CONTENTS

# WHEE, IT'S SPRING!

## The Pickle

Why was I up before dawn?

Earliness and wildness go together. When I was very young, I discovered that the closer to the first gray of dawn I got up and out, the more wild creatures I would see. Our little northern Minnesota town itself was wilder while folks still slept.

One year, morning after morning, just at dawn, seven sharp-tailed grouse flapped and sailed over the rooftops and landed in the big Norway pines down by the schoolhouse while I watched from my bedroom window. My father hunted these handsome wild chickens every fall, and I joined him when I was old enough to fit a twenty-gauge single. So you know the romance was already there when those seven came clucking over town each morning.

Many of my early morning hikes before school were down the Moose Horn River or around Moose Lake. Often on those early hikes I would find deer tracks on the sand beach at the village park. Like ghosts they were; I frequently found tracks but never saw the deer no matter how early I got up. The graceful creatures would tiptoe into town in the predawn quiet to browse on shrubs and maybe snitch a few goodies from the townfolks' gardens.

After the ice went out of the lake, as the days got dramatically longer and the northward rush of bird migration approached its peak, my thin eyelids, seemingly more translucent than most, would let the early light in and signal me that time was a-wastin'. Everybody was up except people. If I didn't get out soon, I was going to miss something very special. Robins were back; warbler waves were coming through; redwings were calling in the cattails.

5

Even as I write this, at six o'clock on a bright May morning, there are, within twenty feet of me, outside the windows where I sit, seven gray squirrels, two red squirrels, a pouches-full chipmunk, flurries of purple finches and pine siskins, a male rose-breasted grosbeak, nuthatches, a chickadee, downy and hairy woodpeckers. They have all come to join me for breakfast. Pairs of wood ducks have been dashing among the oaks and maples and landing on horizontal branches to cock their heads this way and that as they look for good nesting holes. As I glass a male woody and savor the gorgeous iridescence of his dress, I feel the same sense of awe and wonder that I felt as a boy. If maturing means losing that "Wow!" feeling at the grandness of nature, I don't ever want to grow up!

Many special happenings on my boyhood hikes are as clear in my memory as the flashing flights of this morning's wood ducks. Here is one such remembrance:

Two blocks from our home were several adjacent vacant lots along the lakeshore. One bright but cool spring morning I was down there, scrunched in the brush against the low bank, glassing the lake with Dad's old 3x army field glasses. This was in mid-week and fishing season wasn't open yet, so there were no boats on the lake. It was early, three hours before I had to be at school. The town hadn't stirred and the lake was still "wild."

There was no freeway then, and no early morning traffic except the milk truck; the lake was as quiet as Ogishkemuncie or Tuscarora. The sharp whistle of goldeneye wings was the only sound as they swung past; and when they, lesser scaups or any of the three kinds of mergansers landed nearby, I could hear the swish of water as they settled in, followed by the wing flaps and rustles as they re-adjusted their feathers before diving for breakfast. Seeing wild ducks so close that I could watch their pupils dilate was as exciting as life could be to this young birder.

A hawk was hovering at the far end of the lake. The long, bent wings and the obvious search over water told me it was an osprey. Ospreys are sizable birds and uncommon enough to make a sighting very special. Two feet long, with wings spanning five feet, these great fish hawks are ingeniously adapted to do their thing — catch fish. The outer toe of each foot is swung back so that there are two toes forward and two back, the better to grasp slippery prey with those rough scaly feet and sharp strong talons.

In typical osprey fashion it hovered, studying possible prey below, then flew on again as the fish sank out of sight. But several times it sideslipped down to within a few feet of the water, then plunged in, talons outstretched, grasping for a fish near the surface. All tries were misses.

After each miss the osprey would flap free of the water, climb a few feet and shake itself, then climb higher to resume its fishing.

Directly out from me it hovered, dropped a few feet and hovered some more, then slipped left, right, left, right, and plunged!

It sank until just its upstretched wings were above water. Then down they came with a strong flap that should have started bird and fish on a head-first aerial trip to a favorite perch for breakfast.

Instead, there was a commotion on the water that left no doubt that the oversized fish would not come up. The question was, would the bird go down! Flap! Flap! Flap! Splash! Splash!

The big fish wanted no part of going anywhere by air and tried to head for bottom, but the long strong wings of the osprey pumped against the surface of the water and held. Okay, they weren't going down, but they weren't going up either. And ospreys can't breathe water very long without drowning. So the bird had to get its claws unhooked, somehow, fast.

Finally, *finally*, the osprey was loose from its antagonist, which I would guess was just too much northern pike. With considerable flailing and flopping, the long, bent wings at last grabbed some air and lifted the fishhawk from the water. The still-hungry osprey flew to a big pine across the lake to rest for a spell.

I recall an experience from my childhood. I just couldn't get my hand out of the pickle jar — until someone suggested that I let go of that biggest pickle.

# The Breakup

The breakup is a very special time in the north country. Where lakes and rivers are ice-covered half of each year, the reappearance of open water is a major, dramatic change.

Some large northern rivers break loose with so much thunder and show of power that they *demand* a special day of celebration. The very moment of breakup is so sharp and yet so unpredictable that it's a natural for wagers. A timing device documents breakup to the second; TV's are won and sizable bets are paid off. Spring has officially arrived!

I stood on the bridge over the Yellowstone River at Glendive, Montana, one spring just after breakup. I missed the first break, but what I *did* see could hardly be called anti-climax. The roiling water was coming down the contained river bed with awesome speed and power, and was sloshing within two feet of the top of a levee at about roof-top level of many homes just beyond. Great icebergs passed under me and some hit the massive concrete bridge buttresses head-on. The entire bridge shuddered. Sometimes the floes would be upended and show their thickness of several feet. Some quick pencil work gave these battering rams a weight of twenty to thirty tons; no wonder the bridge shook!

No one else seemed concerned so I eventually forced myself to leave, but I'll always remember that super spring show at Glendive.

Spring breakup of Moose Lake, where I grew up, isn't of the magnitude or the crushing force of the Yellowstone or the Yukon Rivers, but even here people have made a contest of it. For many years someone placed an old car on the ice of the lake and attached it to a timer that recorded when it sank. Just about everybody in town and the surrounding countryside guessed the date, hour, minute, and second when the car would drop through the ice; the winner received a substantial prize. In summer they'd cable the old car out and give it a rest until the next year's contest.

One spring day I was on the bridge at the outlet of Moose Lake where the lake water drops over a small rock dam into the Moose Horn River. All summer that drop is hardly more than a riffle, but in the spring run-off a great slurping funnel of water swooshes under the bridge with such volume that we must sometimes lie down in a canoe to keep from hitting our heads as we zoom under the bridge.

It was that kind of a swoosh I was watching at ice-out. A brisk wind was cramming all of the ice into my end of the lake, and the weak, honey-combed ice was breaking into floes. Like a big crowd of people trying to get through an exit after a football game, the floes squeezed together above the dam and then separated and ran as soon as they plunged into the river.

With part of the lake still ice-covered, the ice-cruncher could go on for hours. But like high surf or a campfire, there was a fascination here that held me.

Hey, a *loon*! A single, small square of water had somehow opened a few feet out from the rush of ice over the dam, and a loon from *somewhere* had popped up to fill it. The loon looked wildly about and briefly called its plaintive tremolo, then ducked with a splash just as the opening crunched shut.

I searched for another opening in that vast field of churning floes and thought that the loon should have been taking a big breath rather than calling out just before it dived. I stood on the bridge railing to look for openings farther out, but could see only ice for about a third of a mile. Could it swim that far? Did it know the open water was out there?

There it was again — between two floes just being sucked into the funnel, and splup! down it went in another quick dive.

Several more times that loon played the hair-breadth game of popping up in rare openings and down again as they slammed shut. It was as if it *knew* where the next fissure was going to open and was under that spot waiting.

But finally luck ran out. The wind pushed the floes in so tightly that they did not separate until right on the brink of the slick. The loon disappeared. I watched and waited beyond a reasonable time. No loon. I was quite sure it could not go downstream without my seeing it in that smooth slick over the dam unless it was under a floe. Not likely. I watched for its body to show up as it came over the brink. Nothing. But if it had drowned trying to reach open water, it would be a long time before it would show up at the dam. It would then drift in at the same speed as the ice.

Then a laugh. A loon laugh — way out there. It made it!

Later that afternoon, with the open water in closer, the loon was back above the dam playing the same reckless game. I watched. I was properly amazed. But, this time, I refused to worry.

# The Celebration

I'm not one for hot weather, but warm sun in May — with the ice off most of the lakes and spring flowers putting on their annual show — does feel good! I was camped on an abandoned logging road in northeastern Minnesota near the Canadian border. The chance of another car on that road was about nil, so I parked on the two tracks that were the road and laid out my sleeping bag on the soft white clover growing in the tracks.

Days are as long in May as they are in July. Suppertime seems to come in mid-afternoon with the sun still high in the sky. But my appetite said "feed me!" so I gulped down a quick meal and was soon quietly stalking along the seldom used road.

A recently logged area is not a picturesque scene with its graying stumps and head-high brush; but deer, moose, grouse, and other wildlife like these openings. Sunlight can reach the ground to promote the growth of shrubs, grasses, and other edibles.

This was shortly after World War II; herbicides had not yet been applied to discourage deciduous growth, so this cut-over area was covered with whatever came up. In such a rich supply of food I expected to flush a bear, deer, or moose with every step.

I planned to shoot movie footage for a lecture film so I carried a telephoto-equipped movie camera on a heavy tripod on my shoulder. I was alert with anticipation and "ready for bear!" The stunted grass-clover carpet in the truck tracks cushioned each step. To my hearing, I was making no sound; but even so, I seemed to be the only animal in that big cut. *It ain't necessarily so* that favorable conditions will produce a desired result. But the odds were there, so I continued my silent stalk through the late red light and beyond sundown. It was then too dark to shoot with the slow color film of those days, but that magic time between sundown and dark is when you are most apt to see wildlife. I barely moved; a slow step or two. I watched and listened.

I came to a crossroad, another seldom used clover-grown trail. Here I stopped, eased the tripod off my shoulder, and stood it up in mid-intersection. Resting my crossed arms on the camera top, I remained motionless here until dark, hoping a hunting fox or *some* critter would come along one of the trails and show some curiosity about *me*.

BOOM-BOOM-BOOM-BOOM-BOOM! A kettle drum at forté exploded almost at my feet and the crossroad was suddenly *full* of bouncing rabbits! Showshoe hares were leaping over each other, running under the tripod, and careening in a zig-zag Rite of Spring. The only things missing were the Maypole and the music.

Then, stillness. Absolute silence. The hares, now their summer brown, again blended into the clover in the gray dusk. I waited. Nobody moved. Was this a game? Was I part of it? How long could I hold my breath?

BOOM-BOOM-BOOM-BOOM-BOOM! The big hind foot of a

snowshoe pounded the earthen drum, and the dance was again in full swing.

Several times this happened. (I, of course, thought of Walt Disney's Thumper. It was all there — all but the little humanlike voices.) And why not? Who has more reason to celebrate the warmth and growth of spring than the creatures who slept in the snow at fifty below zero and now are munching the good greens?

I hiked back to camp smiling.

# AIN'T NATURE GRAND!

What is nature, anyway?

To me, it is sunsets and robins' eggs, mountains and blueberries, duckweed, sequoias, and elephants. It is a spring shower, a gathering of penguins, an alpine meadow of daisies, the sparkling moonlight on the South Pacific.

Nature is as small as a grain of pollen and as big as the stretch of space across which starlight that left a distant galaxy four and a half billion years ago is just now arriving at our planet.

Nature is as old as the *Big Bang* that started the universe on its ever-widening flight through space, and as young as a mallard duckling just out of the shell.

Nature is as fragile as an orchid and as rough and tough as an ornery rhinoceros. It is as fast as light and as slow as the growth of lichen.

Nature is my friend. It is the *out-in-the-woods* that I grew up with, the spruce bogs I explored on skis as a boy, the mountains I camped on as a ski trooper, and the back forties and abandoned farms I fell in love with as a planner of camps and nature centers.

---

I like to *experience* nature, to lean against its buffeting winds, to feel its wetness on my face in a thunderstorm or the sting of its driven snow in a blizzard. Deer and birds are out there in it; why not I? A whole season could go by without my full appreciation of its special-ness if I watched it all through windows. So when the best in nature is happening, I want out!

Last night was such a night. It was tree-popping cold. Like random-note modern music on a cracked xylophone, the splitting trees sounded the low temperature. Not a January record by northwoods standards, but minus 37 degrees Fahrenheit was still crisp enough to get me out to feel its coldness.

12

I walked down our forest-walled driveway a quarter mile or so to be surrounded by the cold night. The snow crunched and groaned under my pacs, and nostalgia took me back to the same sounds I knew as a boy in Moose Lake.

I remembered one Christmas Eve it dipped to forty-five below. The cold seemed to make that night even more special as family groups walked — crunch, crunch, crunch — to the small churches scattered throughout our town. Folks were so bundled up we didn't know who they were until they spoke.

Back in those days it seemed that most basketball games and other events at the school took place on brittle cold nights. After the games, people would take the old blankets off their car hoods, pull out the choke, pump the gas pedal, cross their fingers, and press the starter, hoping for a quick catch. Many used hand cranks when electric starters lacked the strength to unglue the cold-thickened oil. Exhaust clouds were white plumes in the headlights, and the snow screamed in agony as tires compressed the granules.

Last night, halfway out to the county road, I stopped and listened. I mentally counted seconds between the sharp reports coming from the frozen trees as they cracked. I never did get to three. No wonder cold country maples can't be used for furniture; every one must be cracked!

Above me the black velvet sky, undimmed by city lights or pollution, held stars beyond count — some brilliant and seemingly close, some so distant and tiny that only the clean blackness exposed them. And beyond those dust-fine mists at the outer reaches of vision were billions of stars I could not see.

Looking at that vastness, trying to comprehend its immensity could be deflating. After all, Earth is just one tiny fleck of dust in that endless space.

And yet, after seeing the marvelous pictures of barren Mars and acid-shrouded Venus, and knowing that every star above me may be as lifeless as those two, I gave silent thanks that I am an earthling. It suddenly hit me that temperature extremes on Earth are not extreme at all. Earth is, obviously, a very livable place.

I strained my eyes, trying to see each tiny glimmer. With so many possibilities for life out there, why shouldn't there be other inhabited worlds?

Well, there may be, but we earthlings have been lucky far beyond rare coincidence. So many great events had to happen *just so* to result in conditions being right for life here, that even *if* other intelligent beings are out there somewhere, we are all so rare in limitless space that none is diminished in importance by the possible existence of others. An inhabited sphere, anywhere, can consider itself unique, and not be far wrong.

Aren't we fortunate, for instance, that Earth just happens to be cruising in an orbit staying about 93,000,000 miles from the sun? The temperature and light at this distance are right for good life here — *as long as we rotate*. Without spinning, we'd fry on one side, freeze on the other. But year after year, century after century, every twenty-four hours, around we go. After a cool night's sleep we swing around to dawn and a gradual warming into a nice bright day, good for work, for plant growth, for a round of golf. And just when it's getting a bit too hot in mid-afternoon to be comfortable, that same steady rotation carries us around to the cool shade of night for evening relaxation and pleasant sleep.

Another bit of luck is that crazy tilt. Add that to our annual trip around the sun, and we get summer growth far north and south of the equator as well as four beautiful seasons.

All of this could be working to perfection, and we'd still be lifeless if it weren't for the marvelous envelope of gas that surrounds our little ball. It would sure be hard to breathe if that gas were other than air, say sulfuric acid, like the clouds that swirl around Venus, or if there were no atmosphere, as on our moon.

Every time it rains it rains — water! How fortunate we are that the abundant liquid on our planet turned out to be water; and that evaporation, wind, and condensation distribute fresh water over the continents.

And thinking of continents, isn't it a good thing that the earth is wrinkled? If it were smooth, our entire world would be covered with water — one huge, shoreless ocean. And we might all be fish.

If gravity on earth were weak, as it is on the moon, imagine the dust storms that would take place with every air movement. On the other hand, a very strong gravity would make walking on two legs impossible. And if we needed four or more legs to hold us up, we probably wouldn't have developed hands, and we might be grazers. As it is, Earth's gravity seems about right. It's strong enough to hold us comfortably down when we're at rest, to hold plates on our dinner table and food on our plates, to contain water in our lakes and make rivers run. And yet we can walk, run, drive, and fly.

The greatest happening of all, the beginning of life on earth, probably wouldn't have gotten a good review if someone had been there to cover the event. The beginning, perhaps around two and one-third billion years ago, was extremely modest; microscopic bacteria and algae in the warm oceans. The world looked much the same as it had before.

But the long evolutionary striving for improvement of species between then and now, the amazing development gained through millions of years of trial and error and natural selection, has resulted in a world that is awesome in its abundance of wonderful life. Every niche that can support life has a plant or creature to fill that niche. And each of those living things, from mold to towering pine, from ladybug to blue whale, is, really, a miracle. Most are beautiful to see. Each is a brush stroke in a painting of the whole of nature.

In nature, specialness is not for a privileged few. Every kind of life is unique, and it is these differences, these *millions* of differences that make living on earth the grand adventure that it is.

Every day we encounter different shapes, colors, sizes, smells, patterns, sounds, designs, textures, and tastes in the natural world around us; and even scientists who are on major expeditions to record new species do not, in their lifetimes, perceive much of all that *is*.

And yet there is so much in *one* forest, *one* swamp, *one* bog, *one* marsh, *one* desert, *one* prairie, that a person could spend a rich, full life exploring a single habitat and know the satisfaction of learning every day. And with the learning, the identification, the interesting facts and statistics comes appreciation of the beauty of it all. That in itself can be fulfilling.

In spring and summer, several ruby-throated hummingbirds come to our sugar-water feeder many times each day. So close we can feel air movement from their wings, we watch from just inches away as the tiny males flare their throat patches as they hover and shift in and out at the artificial flowers. Sometimes the throat feathers are velvet black until they turn toward us; then, like the flash of a sunlit jewel, the red is turned on and so are we by these three-inch charmers.

The ruby-throat's nest is a wee cup less than two inches across, made of plant down, covered with lichens, the whole tied together by spider webs. Like a natural bump on a branch, the nest can easily be passed by when in clear view. We watched a nest in a maple tree visible from one of our windows. Each day we had to search with binoculars to re-discover the nest, about twenty-five feet above the ground. The usual two white eggs are pea-size.

Now all of this is certainly reason enough to like having hummers around. But there is much more. These tiny bits of beauty, looking like metallic green Christmas tree ornaments, have a nice relationship with tube flowers such as the trumpet honeysuckle. The honeysuckle supplies hummers with sweet nectar and tiny insects, and in return the little zippers carry pollen from the anthers of one flower to the stigma of another. Evolution has designed the flower tubes and humming-birds' long bills and tubular tongues to mutually benefit both.

To me, though, the most amazing fact of hummingbird lore is the fall migration of the ruby-throat. Rather than follow a relatively safe land route to their winter homes in Central America, the spunky little hummers take off at dusk on a 25-hour non-stop flight across the Gulf of Mexico, at least five hundred miles over water. The young of the year would never have made this flight before. That these tiny birds, weighing perhaps one-fifth of an ounce fattened up for the trip, can know that Yucatan is across that water, and *fly to it*, is mind boggling.

But even more amazing is the over-ocean mass migration of war-blers and shorebirds from the northeastern states and Nova Scotia across the open Atlantic to the Caribbean and South America. Tracked by radar on the coast, on islands and at sea, one hundred million small land birds choose this eighty-six hour (average) flight rather than a much longer land route. Burning up half their weight, fat stored up each fall to fuel the trip, most of these little one-ounce mites fly the whole way, about 2,300 miles, without rest. Radar scientists say that most of the migrators fly over Antigua at 10,000 to 20,000 feet above the ocean. At that height they are at the freezing point and have only half as much oxygen as at sea level, but they also find brisk tail winds to carry them toward South America.

This magnificent migration, with great "waves" of birds (up to twelve million in one flight), has been watched by up to nine radar stations each fall for six years, and documented in *An Oceanic Mass Migration of Land Birds*, by Timothy C. and Janet M. Williams.

The golden plover flies without rest across twenty-eight-hundred miles of the Atlantic Ocean on its eight-thousand-mile fall flight from northern Canada to its wintering ground in South America. Arctic terns equal a round-the-world flight on their annual arctic to antarctic round trip. Fragile monarch butterflies somehow weather the storms from as far as Canada deep into Mexico and back. Albatrosses and shearwaters that wander the world's oceans return to mere pinpoints of islands where they were born. Salmon find their home stream after years at sea. Green sea turtles range many hundreds of miles from their birth beach, but they find their way back to lay eggs in that same sand.

How do wild creatures attain these abilities to do "their thing" so well?

Nature has no peers in the practice of pure biological science. Every day millions of millions of living things over the earth have offspring. Some vary slightly from their parents. These random mutations can alter in *any* way. Most mutants are probably just a bit different for a generation or two. But a change that for *any* reason improves a species' chances for survival, could cause mutants to live when the "normal" ones didn't make it.

A slightly longer neck on a giraffe, a bit of fatty tissue in a camel's back, a little extra skin between the toes of a duck — all started these creatures toward the superbly adapted species they are today for feeding on high tree vegetation, being able to go long periods without food or water, swimming and diving very well.

The big advantage that nature the scientist has had over man the scientist is time — limitless time. Man can experiment on but few generations of plants or animals during one working lifetime. Nature has "all the time in the world" and has used it to develop the fabulous assortment of living things of today's world.

Murres nest on oceanside cliffs. Their eggs are tapered so they roll in circles rather than off the narrow ledges. They lay only about two eggs each year. I wonder how many murres' eggs rolled off and broke, over how many hundreds of thousands or millions of years, before those that laid tapered eggs became the majority and finally the norm?

Each kind of bird, mammal, insect, plant — every kind of living thing — evolved because there was a niche for it to fill. New plants formed new habitats, new niches. Prey species evolved to eat the fruits of plants; and predator species, to eat the prey.

The whole system of natural selection and survival of the fittest has worked so well that there are now about 8,500 species of birds on earth, 5,000 species of mammals, 20,000 species of fishes, 250,000 species of flowering plants, and 700,000 kinds of insects.

Ain't Nature Grand! is more than just an old saying to celebrate a field of flowers or a colorful sunset — it is an awesome awareness and appreciation of a magnificent world, in a universe that leaves us stunned by its greatness.

# GALLERY I

Finding an arrangement of three pink lady's-slippers at their loveliest, spotlighted by a rare shaft of sunlight in this dark forest, was jackpot luck.

*Saganaga Lake, Minnesota*

Is there a *best* season? I like spring when the hardwood forest around our home is alive with wildflowers. These bloodroots are so trim and neat and fresh, their perfection so fleeting and precious, it almost hurts . . .

. . . Summer's nice too with fresh strawberry shortcake
and corn on the cob, rain on a tent, long pleasant evenings
with maybe a canoe ride, and those gorgeous
doubled-in-beauty northern lake sunsets . . .
*Voyageurs National Park, Minnesota*

. . . And yet I've always said fall is my favorite season.
Flaming colors; soft, soft air; pumpkin pie at church
harvest suppers on clear, frosty nights; football; whirring
grouse; clacking antlers — it's an exciting season! . . .
*Banning State Park, Minnesota*

. . . But so is winter! Winter is so clean and uncluttered. A
curving forest road, a neat farm, even a city home — all are
Christmas-card beautiful after a fresh snow. To ski all
afternoon in an untracked winter scene, then come in
pink-cheeked and hungry to good food by a crackling fire —
that's living.
A *best* season? Ask me at the end of a super day any time
of year, and my answer just might be — NOW!
*Paper birch on Lake Superior's North Shore*

Pioneer plants they are called; lichens, then mosses, the first plants to form on rock after glaciers, fire, or severe erosion have removed all life. The mosses deepen and form soil as they grow upon their own decaying stems and leaves. Finally, seeds are deposited by wind, birds, or animals; and new plants grow, drop leaves and branches to form more soil, starting the long, slow return to forest.

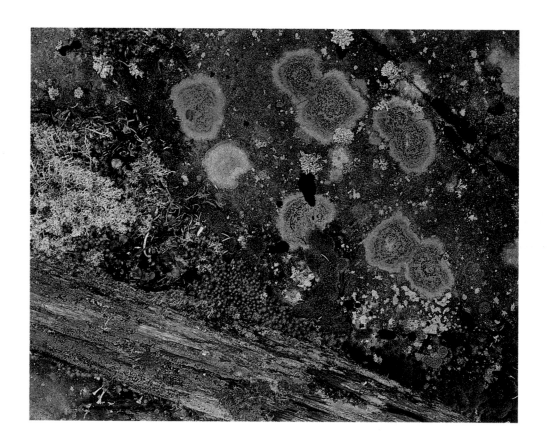

We humans have been presumptuous in thinking of ourselves as *producers*. Our manufacturing processes merely *change* natural materials to suit our needs. The green plant, using the magical effect of sunlight, is the only real producer on earth. The rest of us are consumers.

*Mountain maple leaf, from underside looking up toward the sun*

I had traveled alone far up into Canada's Quetico canoe country in the centuries-old way, by paddle and portage. That was my ticket to this spectacular fall show.

*(Overleaf)*

Misty morning — a fairyland world of alabaster toadstools and delicate crystal chandeliers.

The loon is a bird of wild, northern lakes. Even its mournful call says wilderness.

Like dainty ballerinas, smaller purple-fringed orchis grace
the floodplain along our little stream.

The long, bent wings and the obvious search over water
told me it was an osprey.

Virgin eastern white pines are so scattered and few over
their original range, it makes the great remaining stands in
the Boundary Waters Canoe Area Wilderness in Minnesota
more precious.

# Alaska Sojourn

## The Rockslide

I have been at McKinley Park a month. Son-partner Craig spent a week of that time on the Pribilof Islands photographing sea birds and then joined me here. We have camped on the treeless spongy tundra, experiencing around-the-clock daylight and the famous hordes of Arctic mosquitoes. And we have been getting acquainted with Dall sheep, grizzly bears, moose, and caribou which we hope to photograph in their fall garb.

But this past week has been devoted exclusively to the pikas, the little "rock rabbits" (miniature, round-eared cousins of the cottontail), and their neighbors on the rockslides.

Just now, a pika has padded over the rocks to within inches of where I sit. I actually heard the patter of his furry little feet as he scurried past on his busy farming operation. For he *is* a farmer. He gathers wild "hay" for winter food and stacks it to cure, usually under an overhang, protected from the frequent showers of this mountain country. His "hay" is a much more selective gourmet mixture than domestic stock eat. Many species of tundra wildflowers, shrubs, and grasses are gathered by the mouthful. Any pika is an appealing toy, but this furry little critter with mountain greenery billowing out of both sides of his pixyish face has got to be the superlative of *cute*.

The pika tells you where he is. Sort of. He sits on a favorite rock on the slide and announces his presence with an unspellable high-pitched squeak. I've looked right at that squeak many times without seeing a pika. He is a ventriloquist and may not be where you think you hear him.

He also looks like a little rock if he doesn't move. But continued

37

watching usually discloses the gray mite because now, mid-August, is harvest time, and he scoots around gathering *lots* of hay. Snow could come here in September and cover his home until May, so he builds many haystacks. He adds little bouquets to the stacks each day so that no stack will get too deep with green vegetation and turn sour before it dries.

Craig is to my left, up-valley, waiting for one of the little squeakers to hop up on a lookout rock.

The only sound I hear now is the deep steady gurgle of the small stream hidden in the willows below me. I am comfortably seated on lichen-covered boulders near the foot of a rockslide.

At first look, this steep-sided mountain valley appears bare and sterile. Broad bands of broken rock lie in sloping, varicolored ribbons from the rim of the valley to the bottom of the trough.

Actually, green patches between the slides are lush with tundra and alpine growth, and the slides themselves are many-roomed "apartment buildings," harboring a mixed population of small animals.

A high, steady note lasting several seconds belongs to a hoary marmot calling to alert other marmots that strangers are present. Now he's draped himself like a discarded fur scarf over a rock to absorb as much of the short summer's sun as possible. The marmots gather food from the tundra and down by the stream, but they store it all in their fat bodies because they will hibernate through the long winter.

A mother and three youngsters live in this slide. With slow approach they can be easily photographed. In fact, it's hard not to use way too much film on these constantly posing hams.

The highest pitched call of all, a sharp chirp, comes from the Arctic ground squirrel. These big handsome ground squirrels are numerous almost everywhere in Alaska. It's only natural that they would use the large rocks and boulders at the base of this slide as solid roofs for their tunnels. We watched one pull tall grasses down, hand over hand, to get at the seeds.

Voles, lemmings, mice, and shrews may also be here. I tried to focus on one scurrying mouse-sized creature, but all I got was frustrated.

All of these animals are prey, so you'd think there would be predators around. We have seen a few. A red fox which was neither red, black, nor silver, but a patchwork of colors, came close to us, head down, and meandered through without a pause. An occasional golden eagle floats over, but we haven't seen any interest shown in our little valley.

Two days ago a shorttail weasel showed up, all three ounces of him. Stretching his slender body tall to stare at us, he was as curious about us as we were about him. He held the pose *almost* long enough for us to aim and focus, then dropped into the rock maze to pop up somewhere else, again for too short a time to focus. Warm brown with white underparts, impeccably dressed, this little hunter was alert and handsome. We prized each second of visual contact because those moments were so rare.

To me, the weasels are the biggest predator threat to the pikas and ground squirrels of the rockslide. These lithe little killers can follow them among the rocks and into their burrows, but the rocks would seem substantial protection against most predators. Instant escape routes are everywhere. Eagles would chance a disastrous landing trying to pick a marmot or ground squirrel from among the sharp boulders. And foxes, wolves, wolverines, and even grizzly bears would be laughed at from far up the slide if they tried to dig out burrows in this huge network of rock-lined tunnels.

So life on the rockslide seems to be a ball if one doesn't get caught too far from the rocks when an eagle drifts around the corner, or a fox waits in ambush behind a clump of dwarf birch.

But what about the danger of sliding rocks? They look like they're in almost constant motion, and we just happen to be watching during a brief moment of stability.

Let's look again. Up near the crest there is fresh rock from "recent" slides. Certainly some rock is released each year by the eroding cliffs, cracked and let go by the expansion and contraction of freezing and thawing, washed loose by a heavy downpour, eroded and blown by strong winds, shaken loose by minor earth tremors.

But the lower half, or more, of most slides is gray, not light tan like the fresh slides. Close inspection of these "gray" rocks shows that they are almost totally covered with lichens. Rock lichens spread very slowly. The lichen-covered rocks document decades, even centuries of stability. So the lower ends of the big rockslides are not the dangerous places they might first appear to be, but are, in the lives of many generations of pikas, "solid as rock."

It is now the next day, and a grizzly bear has been here, trying to disprove my assumption that the rockslide would withstand the attack

of any bear. Either last night or this morning the grizzly quarried
enough rock so a person could easily fit into the hole, and stacked the
stones (some of which we couldn't lift) neatly on the rim. The light-
colored lichen-free stones attracted me to the dig. Escape routes for
prey were available in all directions from the hole. It seemed that the
big bear got nothing but exercise for its effort. But a grizzly bear *did*
attack the rockslide fortress. The seeming uniqueness of it made me
look further for other grizzly activity.

I have found another dig. More newly-unearthed stones have led
me to another hole with lichen-free rocks again piled in neat stacks
around the edge. But here, when I look down into this hole, I see not
fresh dirt but well-established sod. This hole must have been dug at
least ten years ago. If these stones have been out in the rain and sun for
ten years or more without even a start of lichen growth visible, how
long have the lichen-covered slide rocks lain here undisturbed?

My whole thinking of rockslide stability must now extend across
many centuries. The soil that covers the base of the slide and is slowly
building between the rocks from the lichens, mosses, and plants that
live and die, documents millenniums of relatively little change.

So the cute little pika, rather than living in a temporary situation
where the next rumbling slide is a constant threat, actually lives in an
apartment complex that may give the pyramids a slow race through
time.

# Stretching the Apron Strings

Across the valley from Craig and me, a big grizzly bear sow and
three large cubs were crossing the steep open tundra. The sow was
staying on an energy-saving contour, but the meandering cubs were
investigating a broad swath. The cubs sometimes broke into a rocking
gallop to keep up.

The mother bear's powerful front legs reached far ahead of her nose
with each step, and her rapid pace was almost frightening in its
achievement. The four slipped into a steep-walled side canyon and out
with hardly a break in stride.

The big bear then angled sharply up the steep green slope a couple hundred feet and immediately began digging. Black earth came flying in enormous volume to either side and between her hind legs. The cubs, almost as large as their mother, ran toward her as if drawn by strings being pulled through a hole, and gathered on the rim of the fast-growing excavation. Crowding their mother, they watched excitedly and even pulled back some sod themselves. In an amazingly brief time a huge mound of earth was piled downhill from the sow, and she was completely hidden in the great hole.

The big grizzly's nose must then have hit a section of tunnel very rich in ground squirrel smell because along with an increased blizzard of dirt came roars of anticipation. That sound alone is enough to make a person thankful that grizzly bears would rather eat alpine flowers than people.

If the bears caught any ground squirrels in that burrow, we'll never know; but they left the hole after a short time, except for one cub who stayed back to sniff awhile. The bulk of the grizzly bear's diet is vegetation — grasses, tundra plants, berries, and roots; but they *do* have a taste for arctic ground squirrels as hors d'oeuvres or dessert. Sometimes they move vast quantities of earth and rock in an often fruitless effort.

From the dig the bears galloped downhill toward the broad band of willows that bordered the creek. Their rippling muscles were very apparent even though they still wore last winter's shaggy coats. They dropped behind the wall of willows, and our eyes slid ahead to where their line of travel should have brought them to an exciting high-splash crossing. Instead, we lost them for a moment.

Then, the tops of the willows on the far side of a thicket began swaying as if in a hurricane. We could follow the movement of the bears by the whipping of the shrubs. What a storm! The entire thicket was in motion. Bears were everywhere, thrashing about, digging, slapping, pouncing. We saw a ground squirrel appear at the stream's edge and run back *into* the willows, probably toward its burrow. That was what this rush attack was all about — dash in and overwhelm them, catch them off guard away from their holes, and grab them in the confusion.

This amazing performance lasted several minutes, with the landscape being altered quickly as five-inch claws tore at the earth. If it wasn't the end of the world for the ground squirrels under those willows, it must have *seemed* like it, with well over half a ton of bears bludgeoning the ground above them. One of the big cubs (perhaps 250 pounds) dashed into the creek, spun to face the shore, and began pulling sod, earth, and rock from the bank.

The flurry suddenly stopped, and the bears crossed the creek below us. They sauntered downstream in a loose line, nonchalant and not even breathing hard. Each bear picked its own spot to climb the steep bank. Before long we saw the four in a meadow high above us, grazing as if the previous exertion had been no more than a peaceful stroll to their pasture.

We checked later and found that the big cub had torn out about twenty feet of ground squirrel runway. If any squirrels were caught, we were not aware of it.

# Love Touch

2:10 p.m. Sable Pass

I just now watched a special moment in nature that I'll try to describe while I'm still warm from the beauty of it.

I have seen one or both of the pair of golden eagles that hunt the Sable Pass area almost every time I've come across the Pass. Sometimes I've been lucky enough to see the long low slanting dive toward a ground squirrel or marmot that usually ends with an upsweep and empty talons. The predatory success rate is always low.

Today the two were drifting along a mountainside, gliding with wingtips just inches from the rocks as they rounded curves in search of prey. This is the way I have most often seen them.

As the lead eagle swung past a cliff, it left the mountain and moved in a climbing circle. Curving back by the cliff, it was a few feet higher than it had been the first time. Buoyed by a gentle updraft, the eagle was starting a quiet soaring climb into the blue. Its mate slipped in under it the second time around, and they ascended easily.

On the third circle the two birds were one exactly above the other, about a yard apart. They were going directly away from me, so I saw the next action very clearly. Suddenly, seemingly as easily as taking a breath, the lower bird rolled to the left until it was upside down. Then, it reached up with its feet, the top bird reached down, and they *touched*. The bottom bird continued the roll-over to the left until it was right side up, and they went on with their circling climb. I don't know if the eagles were as moved as I was by that reaching out and touching, but I almost cried.

*I can relate to that moment.* On a cold winter night when Fran and I are sitting cozily by a crackling fire listening to a symphony or watching a play on television, and an especially moving passage of music or nostalgic moment in the drama causes us to join hands in a spontaneous squeeze, I feel *that* must be akin to the beautiful exchange of those golden eagles.

# The Opportunists

"Sandhills!"

Son Craig and I scrambled out to see. This morning was as wild as the big gray birds themselves. Strong wind had been popping and billowing our tent canvas all night, and this morning gusts were whistling through the willows and balsam poplars of Wonder Lake Campground.

It is mid-September. We have been here since early July, photographing wildlife and scenery. Mt. McKinley and the Alaska Range, towering above us to the south, are already winter-white far down their flanks. We can only imagine the fury of the storms among those rugged peaks.

Migrating flocks of sandhill cranes were circling and calling last evening as the sun, already out of sight, flashed a momentary alpenglow on the peaks. As I went for a late walk in the almost-dark, I heard the cranes again calling from the wetlands on the broad river flats between here and the mountains.

And now, with dust blowing off the gravel bars of the McKinley River in clouds that seem mountaintop high, the big birds are circling again, soaring and calling as if the fifty-mile gusts just make it more fun. Their throaty, burring calls carry literally for miles; you know sandhills are about even before you can see them.

The winds that buffet us down here, where the rolling tundra would tend to cut their force, make the spectacular flight of the cranes seem even more remarkable up in the full gale. We watch with wonder and admiration. Updrafts, invisible to us, seem to be well-marked for the cranes. V after V they come; almost directly above us each

V breaks into a random swarm of circling birds that climb as if on the spiral of a parking ramp. Some circle up to the right; others, to the left in a tight vertical column, making near misses a common happening and crane-watching exciting sport.

As flock after flock join the rising column, hundreds of cranes soar higher and higher in corkscrew circles. Whole groups suddenly disappear from sight as their flat, thin wings point toward us, then just as suddenly flash into view as they swing around so that we see the broad underside of their wings.

When the top birds are just tiny dots, they stretch out again in their long V's, heading east toward Yukon Territory. (Do they find a level up there with less wind to buck, or do they ride the updraft for the sole purpose of gaining altitude so they can "slide" downhill to the next updraft? They do a lot of gliding both in the climb and straight flight, so no matter what the reason, they have mastered the use of air currents to fly their migration routes.)

I suspect that sandhill cranes have figured out how to get a free ride most of the way from the arctic to their wintering grounds in the southwest and Mexico. I've watched them in the Dakotas many times in the fall, and the pattern is always the same — glide downhill for several miles, jump aboard an "up" escalator and climb hundreds or even thousands of feet, then glide again in the direction of migration to the next updraft.

And then do it again. All of this is with very little wing movement. Of course, each bird flaps its wings occasionally, but mostly they are held straight out across their 80-inch span. Compared to migrating redwings or hummingbirds, for instance, in wingbeats per mile the sandhills have it made.

Craig and I have not seen our wives in two and a half months, so watching the cranes head east toward the Alaska Highway helps us decide that we've gotten our pictures. We have decided to migrate with the cranes; it's time to go home!

———————

We're still in Alaska, but about 250 miles east of Wonder Lake as the crane flies, 500 miles by road. Apparently, the Alaska Highway follows a major crane migration route because we've been with the birds all day. Near sunset the late light gave the soft gray feathers a rosy tint. And now, at our night camp, the scattered skeins are silhouettes against a darkening blue sky with a rich apricot glow along the western horizon and a full moon peeking through a group of big spruces on a rugged cliff to the east. All of this — and the only sound in the calm evening chill is the wild cries of the sandhills.

# THE DRUMMER

The hepaticas were lovely, near perfect gold-centered flowers; some bouquet clumps were deep lavender-blue; some, the purest white.

The ruffed grouse ate them anyway. With quick accurate thrusts she snipped them off one by one, leaving the thin stems standing there starkly naked. The short quick movements were made by her head and neck. Her body and legs moved slowly and deliberately. Between thrusts her head was still for a brief second or two, long enough to register the surrounding scene with nearly circular vision. Possible prey for a long list of predatory birds and animals, grouse must be intensely alert to stay alive.

Abruptly, in mid-peck, she stopped. She had plucked only three of a nice clump of eleven blossoms. But there she stood, motionless.

A muffled bass drum sounded uphill to the north — two quick beats, then a slower one, then rapidly increasing thumps until they sounded like an accelerating gas engine on a railroad workcrew's "speeder."

The drumming stopped. The hen, with a purple petal half protruding from the right side of her bill, began a slow-motion stalk toward the source of the sound. Slow step, slide forward; slow step, slide forward. Her body waited until the forward foot was solidly planted, then slowly eased ahead until it was over that foot; then, the second foot lifted and felt ahead for solid, quiet footing.

Twelve minutes later the hen could see The Drummer. The cock was slowly walking along the rounded top of an ancient red oak log. Where the aging wood wasn't covered with green moss, it was barn-wood gray. Most of the bark had long ago dropped off. The damp bottom of the log was gradually turning into humus and settling into the earth, but the still-solid silver topside, with rich green carpets neatly spaced, formed a smooth walkway that the strutting cock claimed as his show-off place. This was his drumming log, and he would defend it furiously against any other male grouse that dared approach it.

Flicking his tail with each step, the cock came to a ridge-growth around a hole where a branch had been. This rough protuberance gave him the purchase he needed for drumming. There, as had many other male grouse during the years the great log had lain there, he turned at a right angle to the log and started to drum.

His short, rounded wings quickly reached out and cupped pockets of air, squeezing them against his breast, PHOOM PHOOM, twice in quick succession, then a slower beat, then a crescendo of beats with blurred wings. Always the pattern was the same. The sound carried a quarter mile or so through the forest, and yet it didn't seem much louder at close range than it had from far down the slope. Ventriloquistic, the sound was hard to pinpoint.

The hen watched, almost totally hidden by shrubs and grasses and still unnoticed by the male. After drumming, the cock crept along the log a few feet, visually searching the forest floor, then turned to go back to his drumming place.

Swoosh! A gray blur swept down across the log as a goshawk dived for the cock. Several grouse feathers floated down as the hawk wheeled for another dive; but the unhurt cock, who had dropped in the lee of the log just in time, was already thundering toward the dense wall of a balsam thicket. Unable to follow with his three-and-a-half foot wingspan, the goshawk perched on an oak branch high above the log scrutinizing the surrounding forest for movement.

There was none. The hen grouse blended into the foliage as if she were leaves and grass. The cock, hidden about ten feet up in the dead interior branches of the balsam thicket, sat quietly against a six-inch trunk and waited for some sign of the goshawk's leaving. A hairy woodpecker clung motionless against the rough bark near the base of a red maple. A white-breasted nuthatch, on another branch of the same oak as the goshawk, froze. *Everybody* froze: chipmunks, squirrels, chickadees — not a bird or small animal changed position as long as the hawk was even suspected of being nearby. Many creatures held still just because they saw others doing so. Somewhere in their ancestry those that moved had been eaten, so now they stayed statue stiff whenever a hawk was about.

The goshawk stayed nearly twenty minutes, then flew silently off through the forest. After another minute of waiting, a downy wood-pecker dared to look around. A chickadee saw it move and hopped to another branch. Soon the hawk was forgotten, and the forest creatures returned to what they had been doing.

Seeing movement and hearing birdsongs, the male grouse fluttered to the ground and walked to the near end of his drumming log. With a jump and two wingbeats he was up on the log and immediately started walking back to his drumming place, raising his soft iridescent green-black ruff and partially spreading his banded tail with each step.

The hen watched quietly from her concealed position as the cock turned to face her and, stretching tall and proud, again filled the forest with his tympani roll. She could feign shyness no longer. Ignoring cover, she walked into a small opening carpeted with last year's red-brown oak leaves that had been pressed flat by the winter's snow.

He saw her at once, flapped down, and ran to within a few feet of her. She turned as if to fly, but immediately turned back toward The Drummer as he stopped and swelled to full display, crest raised and red eyebrows flashing. He raised his great soft ruff to nearly encompass his head and fanned his handsome tail, turkey-like, to a vertical half circle. Partially opening his wings, he banked his body toward the hen so she could see his splendid back feathers as he paraded in grand style around her. Turning his copper-red tail to show off its beauty, he kept it in full fan; the broad black band near the end of the feathers formed a perfect arch.

Moved by this magnificent love dance *just for her*, she quickly succumbed and welcomed the hurried copulation. The hastiness of the love affair did not at all imply lack of pleasure. But more than a few seconds spent in the mating act would have exposed two plump, tasty grouse to a diving or leaping attack by hawk, owl, fox, coyote, lynx, or bobcat.

So the little hen, sexually satisfied for this day, walked carefully back down to her "home" territory near the edge of a beaver pond. There she searched among aspen stumps and shrubs for a hidden place just right for her purpose. Finding a good spot under an old beaver-cut aspen log still attached to its stump, she nestled down into the grass and leaves, turning many times to make her "form" in the shallow depression. Just doing that made a nest-like bed, but she added leaves and feathers to properly protect the dozen or so eggs she would lay.

Each morning after that she visited The Drummer and, as nature worked its wonders, laid a beautiful buffy egg in the well-hidden nest every day until there were eleven. Her last visit to the special log and its champion was a goodbye. Setting, hatching, protecting, and teaching the downy fluff-balled chicks would be her responsibility alone until they were nearly fully grown and scattered in late fall. If she ever saw The Drummer again, it would be an accidental meeting in the forest unless both were alive and in the same area when it came time for mating the following spring.

*It doesn't seem fair, does it?* His Highness plays around on that log for a month or so in the spring, consorting with every hen attracted by his feather drum, and there his parenthood ends. But each hen will willingly risk her life again and again as she protects her young for nearly half a year and teaches them how to survive.

*Fair or not, the system works.* Ruffed grouse cocks have been the drummers, and hens have been the defenders and teachers of their broods since long before man began to philosophize. Slower and weaker grouse are food for a long list of forest creatures; their high birth rate is geared to a great number being eaten each year by predators. Grouse consume many kinds of insects to help keep a healthy balance in forest life, and in eating many fruits they scatter seeds widely. But even if they didn't do any of these worthwhile things, they would still add beauty and excitement to the woodland scene.

# GALLERY II

A magnificent new headdress, a new flowing white mane, the fly problem over, and the cows in season — the high point of this Alaska bull caribou's year is *right now*.

After a brief shower in McKinley Park, a mew gull relaxes
atop a stunted white spruce in the warm late sun.

Dall rams, never far from the haven of cliffs, graze and rest in lush tundra gardens. It seems an easy life, but these same sheep face severe sub-arctic winters on these bare Alaskan slopes.

Sun worshiper extraordinaire, this rockslide-dwelling hoary marmot basks and eats all summer, then completely avoids fighting snow, darkness, and cold by spending most of each year in true hibernation.

Rockslides may look like an unsafe place to live, but they are many-roomed ''apartment buildings'' for small animals. Slow-growing lichens document their relative stability.

Unlike marmots and ground squirrels, the little farmer,
the pika, remains active all winter. Scurrying about in his
rockslide home under the snow, he eats a diet as varied as
in summer, chosen from his many "haystacks" of cured
shrubs, herbs and grasses.

Alaskan mountains defy all superlatives of *large*; the taiga and tundra are literally endless, surrounding the northern world wherever there is land; and yet, the best view of much of the arctic is on hands and knees, especially in September!

The mountain is the mountain. Once you have seen it, you feel its presence even on cloudy days.

*Sunset, Mt. McKinley (Overleaf)*

Camouflaged well enough to disappear almost anywhere
it scrunches down in summer, the willow ptarmigan of the
northern tundra becomes a snowball in winter, except
for eyes, bill, and toenails, and that startling black fan
of a tail that opens in flight and in courtship dances on spring
snow.

A wildlife photographer wants to be close enough to catch the action, but not so close that he gets involved. Alaskan bull moose in early September.
*Photograph — Craig and Les Blacklock*

We had seen this grizzly sow with *three* third-year cubs several times. One day one of the cubs was missing (it was time for all of them to strike off on their own). The big sow, used to being followed by three offspring, stood tall to watch for her third cub.

The cock sat quietly and waited for some sign of the
goshawk's leaving.

Undulating skeins of sandhill cranes sailed above us as we
traveled homeward on the Alaska Highway.
*Photograph — Craig Blacklock*

# INTERLUDE

Late one fall Fran and I took a car trip through the wilds of Ontario. Coming south, east of Lake of the Woods with its fourteen thousand islands, we were attracted by a pine-bordered lake to our left. Never ones to turn down an invitation, we watched for a pull-off and found one with a campsite.

We had time for a canoe ride before dark *or* to make camp. The tip went to the canoe, of course. We would eat a cold supper later and sleep in the back of the wagon. So I slid the canoe off the carrier and onto my shoulders as quietly as possible, slipped it into the calm water, and we were off.

Fran sat and watched while I eased the canoe along the shore. I paddled with a submerged stroke without drip or splash — quiet as a floating feather, a good way to glide up to mink, beaver, muskrat, ducks, moose, or almost any creature that likes shores. We dipped into every bay and barely breathed around each point.

"In the trees!" I whispered. "Against the sky, turkey vultures!" Above us, perched on bare branches in silhouette against the sunset, were a dozen of the most unlikely northwoods birds I know. Oh, they're *there* all right, I've flushed lots of them from northwoods dumps. But they don't seem to *belong*. They're of the desert, the prairie, the south, the stark dead tree by the haunted house.

We watched quietly, then backed off, and continued our shore-hugging search in the silent shadows. Rounding each point was like opening a curtain on a new stage; the action might be only the smooth movement of tree against tree as we glided by; but the clean, moss-garden arrangements of rocks, lichens, plants, and ferns presented a continuous show of wild beauty. The rich deep red of blueberry leaves and the red and gold of bush-honeysuckle against bright green mounds of moss were exquisite.

Widening circles rippled on the mirror ahead. Fran saw them too, so I kept still. *Something* was at the center of those circles, behind that half-submerged boulder. I let us drift — not pushing, merely gliding. Like a floating log, we came around the boulder, six feet out.

It was a mink. He humped up out of the water, shook himself, glanced our way briefly, then moved down the shore, quickly checking every opening between rocks. He disappeared. I eased my paddle to the bottom and gave a soft shove. Just as we reached his exit hole, Mr. Mink came out, a few feet from Fran, and they both stared in fascination. A marvelous moment; then, he was gone.

Darkness sets in early in late fall, and it was time to head for camp. Fran wet her paddle, and we started straight across the small lake, still honoring the great stillness of the wilderness.

"Fran! On the cliff!" I whispered. Fran nodded and watched. On the very top of a rounded granite cliff stood a whitetail buck, quartering toward us, head high, with a great rack of perfectly matched antlers, each with a large extra tine curving out and *down*, to guard his eyes. His attitude was kingly, as if he were aware that he carried a very special crown. We've never seen a more regal animal. Late, rich sunlight bathed the clifftop and spotlighted the buck, completely visible even to his black hoofs. Tall white pines with dark trunks and horizontal plumes of soft green provided the perfect background.

# I Lived with the Deer

Far above my balsam bough bed, birch branches were delicately etched against wispy, silver-white clouds. The nearly full moon seemed especially bright because the translucent clouds spread the moonlight like frosted glass.

Too wound up to sleep, I sat up and slipped my head out of my sleeping bag to listen to the winter silence. Tree shadows curved over the sparkling mounds of undisturbed snow around my camp. It was a warm night, perhaps fifteen above zero F., so I could listen and look for a time comfortably.

I was camped near the Cascade River, about a thousand yards inland from Minnesota's north shore of Lake Superior, in the middle of one of the state's most heavily used winter deer "yards." I was there to make a lecture film on the whitetail deer, to learn what I could about the deer, and to have an adventure.

The adventure was happening already, my first night in camp. The fact that I could be that cozy in midwinter sleeping under the open sky in the northwoods tickled me.

My wife Fran and I had driven up the North Shore Drive that morning; then, Fran returned home with the car. We had been married only three months, but my "desertion" to do this deer documentary was by mutual agreement. Fran knew that this had been a long-time goal of mine, and she was as enthusiastic about the venture as I was.

I had climbed many times to my campsite with enough food and gear to keep me alive, well, and productive for about two months. Choosing a campsite, toting my gear up the hill, gathering boughs and making a bed took all afternoon. The fact that I had flushed two deer on the first trip in and seen many deer tracks and beds while choosing my site was encouraging.

"Hey, what was that? Goldeneyes!" Goldeneye ducks flying over

71

my northwoods camp on a winter night! I should have known they'd be there (several kinds of waterfowl winter on Lake Superior), but in midwinter I'd been thinking deer, not ducks, especially back in the woods. The whistling wings seemed close, but I could see nothing.

Not only was I warm and comfortable in my snug camp, but I felt as secure and confident as I ever would in my life. The likelihood of *any* problem — as long as I was careful — seemed so remote that I dismissed the possibility.

Statistically, I had it made; I was away from cars, houses, and people, so I wouldn't crash, burn, or catch anything. The prevailing northwest wind touched practically no civilization between the arctic and my camp, and it had been screened by about two thousand miles of boreal forest, umptillion needles of spruce, fir, and pine before it got to me. I breathed deep and felt good.

Two years in the mountain infantry in World War II and a boyhood on skis in the northwoods made me feel more at home in that camp than I ever could in a city. I was ready.

My clothing was mostly GI surplus — parka; flight pants; mukluks (those tall, white cloth boots with soft leather "bathtub" soles, layers of burlap innersoles, and wraparound lacings); woolen shirts, sweaters, socks, and underwear; and a ski cap with earlaps.

The mukluks were very practical footwear for cold, dry snow. I usually wore three pairs of wool socks (light, medium, and heavy) and laced the mukluks fairly loose — just tight enough to hold my socks up. All layers were porous so my feet could "breathe," and all of those trapped air spaces kept my feet warm. And yet the mukluks were so light and flexible I felt as if I were barefoot. They were great for working around camp, kneeling long hours on a bough cushion behind a burlap blind, or waiting high in a tree for deer to come within camera range. But I also had rubber-bottomed leather-topped "pacs" for snowshoeing and for wetter snow toward spring.

Food planning for cold weather took lots of time and thought. Everything would be frozen until I cooked or ate it, but I still had lots of choices. (This was in the time before frozen foods were available in supermarkets.) A large metal can with a tight-fitting top held twenty pounds of high-fat hamburger patties, separated by waxed paper so a tap of my axe would break one loose for frying on my little one-burner GI gas stove. The grease from frying a hamburger would immediately freeze so I could cover it and save it in the pan for another meal, perhaps for frying parsnips (often left frozen in gardens through the winter to "sweeten"), or I could split a frozen apple with my axe and fry the two sides face down for dessert.

I craved high-calorie, high-fat foods and ate them in quantity for both warmth and energy. German's semi-sweet chocolate bars were a favorite. I shared them with deer mice, as evidenced by their tiny tooth marks; but the little critters ate so little, I couldn't object. Who could blame them? It was good chocolate.

Winter camping has many advantages. Not only will food not spoil, but there are no mosquitoes, no winter tourists (in those days), and no marauding bears (they snooze all winter). Other critters that might have liked to share my food avoid a human's camp, so only the deer mice helped themselves. I did share crumbs with black-capped and boreal chickadees, red-breasted nuthatches, and gray jays; but that was by invitation. Their visits were pure pleasure — welcome company.

My sleeping bag was an exact duplicate of the one I had used in the ski troops, a thin-shelled down-and-feather mummy bag with an outer bag of the same materials. I could sleep in either one or both, depending on the temperature. I would automatically slip deeper into the bag as the temperature dropped, leaving just enough opening to breathe. I knew from comfortable nights high in the Rockies that I needn't suffer in temperatures to fifty or sixty below zero F.

I had winter-camped under lean-tos made of evergreen boughs, in tents, in snow caves, and in the open. On this adventure I wanted to be able to see in all directions from my bed and to hear the night sounds clearly, so I camped under the open sky. I made a bough bed on the north edge of a small opening in the forest, protected from north winds but exposed to some warming sunlight on bright days, to help freshen and fluff my sleeping bags.

With foam pads and air mattresses now in vogue for outdoor winter sleeping, bough beds are out. With so many winter campers, that's probably a good thing for the forest; but picking just the tips of lower branches as I did, the effect was hardly noticeable and would be hidden by the next year's growth.

A balsam bough bed can be very comfortable, or it can be a pile of sharp sticks. I picked only flat springy fourteen-inch or so boughs (they snap off easily in cold weather), and I threaded them onto a three-foot stick with an upturned stub of a branch at the bottom. I could pack what would have been a number of armloads of loose boughs onto this stick, and with several loads have enough for my bed.

I shaped a basic bed of snow to make a firm, level base; then, starting at the head of the bed, I stuck the butt ends of the boughs straight down into the snow in a tight pattern with each bough curving toward the head of the bed, with the soft ends overlapping each other like feathers on a turkey's breast. The resulting bed was springy and fragrant, and lasted my entire stay.

I had a tent with me but, of course, did not intend to use it unless it rained. And I *could* build a fire, but one tends to hug a fire when it's cold rather than to adjust to the weather with proper clothing, food, and activity. Tending a fire takes valuable time and gets one used to the warmth, so it *seems* colder away from the fire. So I planned to live with the cold. That way I would be as comfortable in a blind or a tree as at camp.

The first morning a constant roar from Lake Superior told me that ice fields were jamming against the shore. I felt compelled to go down and see! My clothing was warm and dry between my inner and outer sleeping bags so I could dress in reasonable comfort. A few cookies (a dandy way to eat oatmeal in a winter camp) made a quick breakfast, and I was on my way.

When I reached the lake, I could see ice to the horizon; and it was *all* coming to this shore! The crushing, grinding breakup was possibly a hundred miles or more broad, the ice forced against the rocks by wind pressure on hundreds of square miles of surface. The immensity of it and its unstoppable power were awesome. I felt as if I wanted to find a phone and call *everyone* to come and see!

*The impossible was happening:* an irresistible force was pushing steadily against an immovable object, neither giving in to the other. The ancient Pre-Cambrian rock cliffs, slopes, and boulders didn't budge as the ice field kept coming. And the ice field was moving just as fast as it had before it hit the shore, not slowed a bit by solid rock. The crushed ice piled higher and higher, but the field was unstoppable.

Back from the lake the overall sound was a roar, but near the shore I heard grinding, sliding, breaking, tinkling. The clear inch-and-a-half-thick ice seemed glasslike as it rose up and broke, piling pane against pane like fallen dominoes, far out into the lake. The likeness to breaking glass almost made me feel uncomfortable, like accidentally kicking a football through a stack of storm windows.

The next day the big lake was ice-free. Long, flat swells rose and settled almost imperceptibly, obvious only because of gentle sloshing on the gravel beach where yesterday's ice had mysteriously disappeared. A flock of about two hundred old-squaw ducks far offshore shouted very important messages to the world. The shouting diminished as the flock dived until the very last duck gave one very last (but most important!) exclamation before it went under. The sudden silence was eased a bit by the pleasant swooshing sounds of the beach-edge swells.

After a seeming lung-bursting time under water (they can dive 100 feet or more), one old-squaw reappeared and came up shouting. As each duck surfaced, the din increased until the convention was again in full swing.

I love that shore. When there were storms, I often went to the shore to experience each one full blast, to stand on the treeless rocks and welcome the sting of flat-driven snow on my face, to hear the KA-WHUMP and feel the spray of mountainous waves against some of the oldest rock on earth.

I was careful to stay on top or on the landward slope of the rocks. To start sliding on spray-built ice toward the cliff-edge and into the wild wet was frightening just to think about.

I saw deer every day, often the same deer at approximately the same place day after day. Many deer stayed near the lake, especially at night. The warmer-than-air lake tempers the climate along the shore, making it many degrees warmer than a short distance inland. One motherless yearling often spent the night in a shrubby thicket just a few feet from the shore rocks. Curled up like a doughnut with one ear sticking up from the middle, she slept quite soundly in her comparatively warm nest.

I was standing in the trail one day, on my way back to camp from the lake, when I noticed a deer coming down the trail toward me. It hadn't seen me so I placed my back against a tree and slowly slid to the ground. Seated there, braced against the tree, I could hold rockstill.

The deer kept coming, pausing only to nip an occasional mountain maple twig. About thirty feet from me it noticed me, cocked its ears forward, and stared hard. I barely breathed; a wisp of vapor would give mc away. Truc to thc book, the deer didn't believe its eyes. Shaking its ears, it browsed a bit more, coming closer with each step.

At eighteen feet it looked again, flicked its ears again, browsed again.

Fifteen feet from me it stopped dead, legs spread, and stretched its neck toward me — staring, listening, and sniffing. It *still* didn't believe I was for real! Even that close, the deer was tempted by a nice red twig.

It swung its head but didn't reach the twig because it had to stare at me some more. Three times it reached for the twig, and three times it swung back to eyeball me. On the fourth try it nipped the twig, then munched away as it watched me, calm again.

I halfway expected the deer to step over me, but it didn't. At about twelve feet it left the trail to walk around me, keeping about that far away. Opposite me it got my scent, made a turning leap, and went bounding off, tail up, whistling with each bound; WHEW ! WHEW! WHEW!

One night it was quite warm, up in the twenties. I had undressed my bottom half and put it to bed, but my top half was still parka-d and up, reading. I was on one elbow, enjoying a cold adventure in the Alps in *White Tower* by James Ramsey Ullman. An electric lantern hanging from my tripod provided a bright spot of light on my page, making the surrounding darkness seem absolute. A pattering of corn snow was falling, but it either bounced off the pages or rolled off when I tipped the book.

A low moan came from up inland. I stripped off my parka hood and ski cap and fine-tuned all senses. The next note was higher, but still baritone. The third note of the male timber wolf duplicated the second, but was joined by a soprano obbligato from his mate. There apparently were only the two wolves, but I doubt that I have ever been so thrilled by, or appreciative of, any concert. That was the first time I had heard timber wolf music. Succeeding times have left me no less impressed. That harmony is so beautiful; the occasion, so rare.

----

It was one of those late winter snowstorms — big goosefeathers almost touching each other. You could watch the marshmallow mounds grow on balsam boughs. The quietly falling flakes and the deep, soft snow pillows hushed all sound.

I hung my sleeping bag over a protected branch to fluff, made sure a heavy tarp was covering food and gear and another tarp covering my bed, and headed inland, up into the Sawtooth Range on snowshoes, exploring and deer watching. I knew that the deer concentrated near the lake for warmth, for the cover of the cedar-spruce-balsam thickets, and for avoiding the deeper snow inland. But I didn't know how far up the hill these changes took place on the Cascade River, so I went to see.

Near camp I glimpsed the usual tail-down sneaking exits as deer, having seen me first, slipped away. But within a few hundred yards tracks and beds disappeared, and I saw no more deer.

The snow was much deeper up there. There seemed to be no wild-life of any sort, at least in that snowstorm.

I came to a tennis-court-size opening in the forest. A fine white spruce grew in the center with branches weighed down and almost hidden under new snow. My uphill exploration would lead me across the opening and right by the handsome spruce.

Sometimes I feel a twinge of guilt, putting a man track through a lovely scene. But a snowshoe track sort of *belongs*; after all, Indians have snowshoed this country for hundreds of years. My track would soon be covered anyway. So I started across. One thing about it — a lone man isn't talking to anybody, so I didn't disturb the beautiful soft silence. I was within a few feet of the tree, when —

WOOSH! the base of the spruce exploded right next to me. Branch-es sprang up and snow flew off as four big bucks arched out in four directions. I was almost run over as the one on my side burst out, breaking the branch barrier that had lowered around the dozing bucks. They were almost in an igloo. No wonder they didn't hear me coming.

So *that* was where the big bucks lived. *Of course*. Staying deep in the boonies is how they get to *be* big bucks!

# MIDNIGHT MEETING

One of my favorite camping places is the site of a northern Minnesota 1930's CCC camp. All traces of buildings have been gone for years, but the good grass is reluctant to let the surrounding forest invade, so the openings remain, and wildlife likes to come around.

I've seen bears there, and moose, and had a field day with a Cape May warbler that led me frustrated around a trio of willow clumps until at last it posed among the yellow catkins against the blue. It's also a good spot for ruffed grouse. On spring evenings the woodcock dances there, flying straight up beyond all reason before its seemingly suicidal dive back to its starting point, slamming on the brakes just short of disaster. I don't know how impressed the hen is with this performance, but I am, very!

There's a great rock ridge that starts near that campsite and climbs to a super vista with a view over thousands of acres of wilderness. You can see the Canadian border cliffs from there. Behind the ridge is a beaver lake where I got a movie shot of a fisher many years ago.

So you can see why I'm drawn to the old campsite again and again to work with my camera.

Late one night in May I left the North Shore Drive of Lake Superior and started driving inland on the narrow dirt road to this special place, wide awake and with juices flowing, expecting wildlife around every curve. That time of year around midnight the road is used more by wildlife than people.

Jackpot! A rare treat. A long-legged mop-footed Canada lynx showed in the headlights and trotted along the right edge of the road as I slowly followed with the camper. When I got too close, he slipped behind roadside grasses and I lost sight of him.

A bit farther up the road the biggest member of the deer family ever to walk the earth stood broadside before me. I drifted in reasonably close to admire the great black bull moose. His dully glowing eyes stared back. He milled around a bit. I thought he was confused by my lights so I turned them off to give his eyes a chance to readjust to the darkness.

After a bit, expecting the bull to be gone, I again pulled the headlight switch. He was walking down the road toward me. I immediately doused the lights and waited. On again; he was still coming! I started the engine, slapped the truck into reverse, and started backing.

The bull kept right up with me. At five feet per step his steady walk ate up ground as fast as I dared retreat. The Wild Goose didn't have back-up lights so I was guessing where the road went. On he came, right between the headlight beams.

Finally he zeroed in on my left headlight. I slammed on my brakes, jammed into a forward gear, and swerved out and around the bull. I could have brushed his entire length with my left hand as I roared by him.

Now you know and I know that a bull moose is usually an unaggressive animal in the spring. His antlers are tender and only about a third grown, and the rut doesn't start for another four months. But we also know that bull moose have attacked railroad engines. So when this twelve-hundred-pound critter acted as if he were going to walk right up on my hood, I wasn't *about* to discuss seasonal activities with him.

# FEATHERS IN THE FOG

Northern Light Falls is an intimate place. The waterfall is little more than a rapid between two lakes although one summer a canoe that was wrapped around one of its rocks discouraged would-be-rapid-runners.

Nevertheless, the relatively small waterfall and the coziness of the site itself tend to make it an ideal one-person campsite. There are clean, weather-washed rocks below the high water line, and lichen-painted boulders above. It is an open happy place, exposed to the sun most of the day. You can live with yourself for a bit and practice a little Waldenism.

Late September/early October is my favorite solo canoe-trip time. The crowd has gone home, and fall color is at its best. One October evening I had eaten a substantial supper by the falls. Warmly dressed in wools against the evening chill, I sat by the lower lake, with chin on knees, waiting for a beaver to return to finish cutting a five-inch aspen. Twenty feet from the tree, I'd have a good look at this operation.

Beavers don't come. They're just suddenly *there*, as this one was. Something drew my eyes to the flat water in the dimming light. There it was, a black form on black water, absolutely still. Curving surface-tension around its body caught the pale sky and etched its shape in a thin white line.

I was in the open but as still as a stump. Only my eyes moved. What patience the beaver had! He lay there for minutes, log-like. Finally a twitch. Then propulsion. He swam in close below me, then slowly circled a broad loop, his head pushing up a smooth curve of silver which trailed back and out in a graceful V.

Once he decided the coast was clear, he went right to his work, climbing the few feet to the aspen, standing up to the tree, tipping his head to one side to make a wedge-shaped cut and chewing away. Not a big animal, the two-year-old may have been a loner, or its mate was logging elsewhere.

> The big upper incisors look like the chisels in a beaver's set of cutting tools. But, like all of us mammals, it's his lower jaw that is hinged, and it's the lower teeth that slice out the chips.
>
> Mostly, beavers are aspen eaters, and their staple diet is the inner bark of those soft trees. When the aspens are all logged off from the beavers' woodlot, they may leave in search of another aspen forest. But the fat loggers will also eat birch, alder and willow. I've seen many beaver dams and lodges in high mountains where the only food and building material available was head-high willow shrubs. On several occasions I've seen iron-hard red oaks cut by beavers where aspens were plentiful. Show-offs!

My friend munched on the aspen. The tree was on a slope, and he couldn't find good footing on the downhill side, so he just chewed away from above. Normally he would chew equally all around until the tree fell. This aspen, near the shore, was leaning out toward the open lake, reaching for sunlight as all trees do. When Mr. Beaver severed enough fibers, down went the tree into the water.

> Because *all* leaning shoreline trees drop into the water when beavers cut them, some people think that beavers can *make* trees fall any way they wish. The truth is, the beavers just cut the trees; if they're leaning over water, that's where they will drop. Back inland, beaver-cut trees drop every which way. Many lodge against other trees and are unreachable. If the beavers had any control over direction, they certainly wouldn't do all that cutting for nothing!

I waited in the growing darkness until the beaver did some limbing and cut off a small log to tow to a favorite spot for "breakfast." Then, I quietly moved to my tent and the welcome warmth and coziness of my sleeping bag. I'm sure he never knew I was there. I expected the entire aspen, a small tree, would be cut up and stored on the lake bottom as part of his winter food supply, by morning.

Loons do not sing in the fall. But the possibility of hearing the grunting challenge of a bull moose or the howling of timber wolves makes night listening exciting. Hearing just the small waterfall, and knowing that I was the only person in many square miles, sent a warm tingle through my body. Sleep took over quickly on that frosty fall night.

Dawn was foggy gray. I slowly and quietly raised to a sitting position, keeping my bag tight around me, and pulled my knees up to rest my arms on them. Warm and comfortable, I could watch the day come without disturbing its wildness. There is no need to close the screen in October, so the front of the tent was wide open.

I had visitors. Two ruffed grouse were dark forms moving silently among the mountain maple clumps. They entered the short-grass, clover "yard" of the campsite and came toward the tent, plucking clover leaves and blossoms. Gradually the feather patterns became discernible as they meandered closer in the dim light. The dark banded tails — one gray, one red — flicked open into broad fans as the birds suddenly were aware of the change in landscape. Their ruffs fluffed into full circles, and their crests raised with each cautious step. Curious, they stood tall to look right at me from about eight feet, then nervously retreated into the fog.

They continued to fan their tails and ruffs as they moved out onto a thin granite point in the lake above the falls. An arching branch above and the grouse on the rock became an oriental silkscreen print, gray-on-white. The entire scene was duplicated in flawless reflection.

As soon as the birds reached the end of the visible world, they flew, *without a sound*, into the white nothing. Some faint circles on the surface of the water documented for a moment that it had really happened. Then water and sky became one again.

# GALLERY III

The fragrant water lily unfolds each morning to display its lovely gold treasure.

*The Theater of Seasons*, the north country is often called. With a temperature difference sometimes of 150 degrees F between midsummer and midwinter, plants, birds, and animals that are out in that vigorous climate must be pretty vigorous themselves to survive.

The *only* way to get here in summer is by canoe.
*Quetico Provincial Park, Ontario*

I saw deer every day. Many of them stayed near the lake;
the climate was warmer and the snow shallower than
inland.

Coyotes hate to sing alone. Almost always, when one
starts, others join in, in a yipping, howling chorus.

Moosehide moccasins padded by Little Rock Falls on the
Canadian Border long before the white man came here.

The Boundary Waters Canoe Area is now protected by
wilderness status.

*(Overleaf)*

One of my favorite solo campsites, Northern Light Falls,
where two grouse visited my camp that foggy fall morning.

When I was very young, there were lots of woods and not
many people in the country near our town. One spring
ritual was *picking* the very fragrant trailing arbutus. We
know better now.

*This* gold doesn't vascillate in value. It is priceless for a few days every fall.

There had *better* be owls! Their chief prey — voles, mice, and shrews — can have as many as *seventeen* litters in a year. Without owls, we'd be up to HERE in voles!

"Me? Swipe your sweet corn? Never happen! Nobody as adorable as I am could ever do anything naughty. — Well, I might *borrow* some."

The blackwing damselfly is, whether male or female, every
millimeter a graceful, delicate lady.

# The Naughty Little Boys of Birddom

Crows are sleek compared to ravens. Raggedy ravens, loose-feathered and about twice the bulk of crows, still may be taken for crows at a distance. If a big, black, crow-like bird soars, it is most likely a raven. If it croaks, screams, and rattles, it *is* a raven. Watch that bird. Before long it will do *something* to entertain you, whether it means to or not.

---

It's a rainy summer day here at Teklanika Campground at McKinley National Park. I'm wearing wools because it's cool, but to hear the plaintive pitiful cries of the half-dozen ravens in camp, you'd swear they're all about to die of malnutrition and hypothermia if someone doesn't toss some good, calorie-rich food out to them *right now*!

Don't believe 'em. They get along fine in January with deep snow and sixty below so their pretending starvation at this lush season is a put-on.

But that's ravens. They tease, cajole, pester, play pranks, steal (Don't tell *me* they don't know what that means!), and make fun. They are jokesters supreme, making a fool of you and then laughing with glee. And they are one of my favorite birds.

Last night at a campfire lecture (It's too light even at midnight up here to show slides.), everyone was laughing as the lecturer, a woman ranger, held up a caribou skin. Now that action isn't particularly funny, so she swung around just in time to see a camper racing toward his open-topped pack a little too late to keep a raven from flying off with what appeared to be a sandwich. The camper had come in from a hike.

101

He saw the lecture in progress, grabbed a bite, and came over to listen. The raven saw the unsecured cover on the pack and helped himself.

---

Ravens are the otters of the bird world. They'll play games at the rise of an updraft. Son Craig and I watched a spectacular show as dozens of ravens climbed, dived, circled, stalled-out, tumbled, and barrel-rolled at the edge of the Grand Canyon on a strong wind coming up from the depths.

Turkey vultures circled on that up-blast too, but they didn't seem to have nearly so much fun. Super-soarers, vultures give one the impression that they could stay aloft on the rising air above a candle flame. With their broad, six-foot span in a low V, tipping delicately right or left to best use gentle thermals, turkey vultures can float above warm earth on the calmest days.

You'd think they would have cut up a bit on the vertical winds along the walls of the Grand.

But no. The big black buzzards couldn't seem to bend from their ghoulish, circling, search-for-death image. While the playful ravens dipped and dived all around them, the somber vultures slowly wheeled and drifted along the wall. I felt like shouting, "Hey, you guys, join the fun!"

---

Wife Fran and I watched two ravens tumbling above the cliffs on Upper Michigan's Keweenaw Peninsula. They circled higher and higher until they got enough empty under them for a spectacular fall. Then they clasped feet a la eagle aerial courtship and tumbled like a broken umbrella until almost too late, pulling out just above disaster. Then they circled up to do it again.

---

One beautiful blue day in the first week of May, I was standing near the outlet of still snow-covered Chilkoot Lake near Haines, Alaska, enjoying the first warmth of spring. A black dot flying the length of the lake toward my end turned out to be a raven, and it swung over my way, seemingly when it saw me. There were just the two of us. So I stood waiting and watching.

About a football field away from me the raven flipped over and flew on his *back*! At the same time he let out a good strong raven croak, presumably to make sure I saw this remarkable performance. Then he righted himself and kept coming. Almost over me, he turned over again, squawked at me, flipped back upright, and flew on down the Chilkoot River.

I looked all around. There wasn't another bird, person, or animal present that I could see. I had to believe that grand display of aerial dexterity was just for *me*.

———————

Grant Hagen, Jackson, Wyoming, wildlife artist, told me a raven story that says it all. He had a pet raven that had gotten the dander up of every dog in town.

It seems that this raven delighted in tweaking the tails of sleeping dogs. It also seems that dogs don't really like to have their tails tweaked at nap time. So there was no love between the raven and Jackson's dogs.

One day a dog was slinking along the side of Grant's garage. Around the corner in midyard was the raven, asleep. Grant watched with great interest. It looked like some tables were turning.

The dog reached the corner, readied every muscle for the quick dash, then streaked across the lawn toward the sleeping bird. A short spring and he had him — almost. A fraction of a second before teeth hit feathers, the great wings opened and with a couple of flaps lifted the bird just above the out-of-control dog. The dog roared under the bird and, embarrassed *again*, continued on home. The smirking raven gently settled back into the soft grass to continue his "nap."

# THE CONTRIBUTION

Two ravens played high in the sky over the rugged Minnesota-Ontario border wilderness. It was a warm, blue day in March. The temperature was several degrees above freezing, but the dazzling white snow on the lakes and in the forest reflected the sun's rays and stayed cold and fluffy. And yet icicles were forming at the tips of snow-draped evergreen branches; balsam needles, dull brownish green all winter, were turning bright green again; and open water around the rapids was broadening. Spring was on its way.

Perhaps seven or eight hundred feet above the hills and cliffs two ravens played tag and showed off with spectacular barrel rolls, tumbles, and swoops. They squawked, croaked, rattled, and screamed, letting the world below know that *something* was happening up there, though non-raven ears might have trouble discerning among raven joy, rage, and pain.

Suddenly one of the ravens hovered for a few seconds, then folded his wings and dived straight down. Bullet-like, he dropped two hundred feet in seconds, then curved back up in a long smooth arc, stalled out, dropped again, and repeated the maneuver. Descending in loops, the raven was soon circling just above the treetops, talking gutteral words of importance to his mate who had followed him down.

The two landed in a tall big-tooth aspen, quickly dropped to some small quaking aspens below, then with surprising agility flapped down from branch to branch until only open space separated them from the deer carcass lying on the snow.

They, of course, had seen the two timber wolves lying in the sun on the next ridge — the big young male sprawled on his side, sleeping soundly; the smaller female, head on paws, alert but resting easily.

The pair of wolves had come upon the old buck shortly before dawn. The story written in the snow told of the brief struggle. The ten-year-old deer was close to starvation. His tracks showed where he had wallowed a short distance from a trail to search for nourishing red shoots among the thick gray stems of mountain maple. All of the tender young shoots were browsed to mere stubs or were above his reach. The wolves had found him there, and he had not had the strength to bound away.

The male wolf had eaten about fifteen pounds of venison; his mate, about ten. It would be many hours before the pair would have enough appetite to go back for a second meal. The female heard the ravens' comical conversation as they discussed their find, but she was too stuffed to care.

From their low perches the ravens studied the carcass briefly. Two chickadees and a gray jay were pecking at the meat, but they flitted to nearby shrubs when the first raven flapped down. He landed on hard snow that had been packed by the feasting wolves, and walked around the buck. His iridescent feathers were shining, and his neck was fully ruffed as he appraised the free dinner. His mate joined him; and, quiet now, they began some exploratory pecking. The female poked at some marrow where the big wolf had broken a femur. Reddish and softened, the marrow had already been drained of its rich fat by advanced starvation.

The chickadees and gray jay came back and snatched bits from the far side as the ravens found choice cuts. Around sunset the birds left for their varied roosts, to huddle together and fluff their feathers against the night cold.

Shortly after dusk there were no visitors at the carcass. But as darkness deepened, several small forms scurried from holes in the snow to the deer, then quickly back to their holes with a prize. Deer mice, mostly seed eaters, gladly added venison to their diet. One little scurrier ended up *being* a prize as a shorttail weasel intercepted it near its burrow. The weasel ignored the venison. It prefers fresh meat, or at least meat that it has killed.

As a full moon rose high enough to bathe the carcass in the brightest possible night light, the deer mice retreated to their runways under the snow. Owls hunt well enough on the darkest nights. Moonlight excursions could be suicidal.

A red fox sat quietly in deep shadow under a snow-draped balsam, staring at the deer. For perhaps twenty minutes it watched. Then it crept forward into the moonlight, stopped in mid-stride, stared, and listened. Its nose twitched. Another few soundless steps, it stopped again.

The fox's meal was furtive. The night cold had frozen the meat so every bite had to be gnawed free. The fox stopped every few seconds to look and listen. It stayed at the carcass for more than an hour, worrying small bits of meat loose and never relaxing its vigil.

Suddenly, it raised up — all senses straining and focused; then it immediately slunk in a low crawling trot back to the deep shade under the balsam. There it again sat and watched through the canopied branches as the wolves returned to their kill.

Far from ravenous, the wolves were back more for a snack than a meal. They romped in the soft snow for several minutes before they started picking at the carcass. They both chewed on bones for a while, with cracking and gnawing sounds easily heard by the waiting fox. Then the female chewed on a bit of hide while her mate worked at removing a leg. For more than two hours the wolves enjoyed a leisurely lunch. Finally, ready for change, they stood up, pawed playfully at each other and licked faces a few times, and trotted off, the male carrying the leg to bury in some secret place.

The fox chewed at the deer the rest of the night. The accumulation of his patient gnawing added up to a sizable meal. He would sleep well the following day.

The next morning, shortly after sunrise, seven ravens were on or around the carcass. By afternoon there were thirteen ravens. Several more gray jays appeared, and some boreal chickadees joined the blackcaps. Two saucy mites, red-breasted nuthatches, came to the party around noon.

In mid-afternoon a golden eagle noisily flapped down to the open snow where the wolves had played, then walked awkwardly to the carcass. Spreading its seven-foot wings and its ruff and snapping its hooked beak as it approached the deer, the eagle immediately dominated the pecking order. All of the ravens flew to surrounding trees, then left as the eagle showed its displeasure of any attempt to share the deer.

A red squirrel churred from a white spruce. He wasn't a serious competitor for the venison, but he shouted out his two-cents-worth anyway. A few moments later he was under the snow fetching a cached cone. Then he sat on his favorite low branch, husking out the seeds and covering the snow beneath with red-brown scales.

The temperature was in the mid-forties. The snow became soggy and started to settle. It had been fluff clear to the ground all winter.

Ruffed grouse would be blocked for the first time from diving into warm snowbeds when the snow froze at dusk. They'd have to roost in trees as they do in the snowless seasons.

The dark deermeat absorbed warmth from the high sun and thawed where it was exposed, so the eagle could use its great beak and strong feet to tear off sizable bites. He gorged an awesome meal, as is the way with predators, until his added weight would make his take-off labored. He waddled to the opening where he had landed, then thrashed away at the soft spring air. His feet pushed down hard three times, trying to force the body higher, but sank deep into the thawing snow instead. Three broad sets of wing patterns on the snow marked the take-off; on the fourth flap just the right wingtip touched as the eagle banked to gain the open sky. Staying in low gear with engine racing, he angled slowly upward to a tall white pine, where he grasped a strong horizontal limb, probably did an eagle version of a burp or two, and settled down to turn some deer steak into eagle muscle.

For five days there were only brief moments when the carcass wasn't being eaten by *something*. The visitor list was almost a complete Who's Who of the northwoods creatures that depend on predators to make protein and fat available for their winter diet.

There were, of course, the predators themselves — the two wolves. They returned on the third night for a last big feast, then buried the best remaining parts for future use, tamping the snow with their noses. By the end of the fifth day, when fresh snow covered the few bare bones that were left, the carcass had given sustenance to: 27 ravens, 8 black-capped chickadees, 5 boreal chickadees, 3 red-breasted nuthatches, 7 gray jays, 2 wolves, 1 fox, 11 deer mice, 1 pileated woodpecker, 3 downy woodpeckers, 2 hairy woodpeckers, 1 black-backed woodpecker, and 1 golden eagle.

During his lifetime the buck had sired somewhere between ten and forty fawns (depending on his dominance, the ratio of bucks to does, and the number of deer in the area).

Each winter for nine winters the buck had dropped two antlers in the snow. And each spring those antlers disappeared quickly as rodents ate them for the calcium they needed to grow strong bones and teeth.

During his long life the buck had applied rich manure over his range, fertilizing the plants which give food and cover to wildlife and produce the oxygen we all breathe.

The chain of life goes on, not only in the buck's descendants but through the female wolf to her robust pups, and through all of the creatures who fed upon the deer, to their young. As in all of nature, life did not stop when the buck's heart stopped, but continues in an unending flow of vigor and beauty.

# THE CHALLENGE

The Yellowstone Park pronghorn buck was about forty feet from me, broadside, but looking away. I was close enough, my camera was focused, and the picture composed. I would ask only one more thing: would he *please* swing his head around to look off to my right rear? That would be the classic pose, body angling away, head turned partway back toward the camera.

I'm sure he heard me. I'd been trying to talk him into the move for several minutes after a couple of hours of slow open stalking to gain that closeness. The picture on the ground glass of the old 4 × 5 Graflex was really not bad, and I did squeeze off a couple of shots to document the scene on that balmy October afternoon. It's just — you know, if you had your dibs.

The buck started walking in the direction he'd been staring. I had to let him go because I couldn't do anything to hold him. I whistled, waved a handkerchief. He would have none of it. He had accepted me as a fellow grazer. What more did I want?

Only then did I look out across the valley in the direction of his stare. Across the Gardner River on a flat plain was a herd of about twenty does and fawns, and one sizable buck. So *that* was it. My buck had been talking himself into a confrontation with the herdmaster.

The psyching-up had taken a while; but once the decision was made, he was committed. His determined pace took him straight down the steep slope into the ribbon of juniper that hid the river from my view.

I knew there was a rushing stream of belly-deep white water down there, and my image of pronghorns has always placed them in dust-dry sagebrush desert; they're not what you'd call amphibious. But there he was, climbing the bank on the other side of the river. He obviously was not bluffing. The contest was just seconds away.

I followed the buck to be as close as I could be to the coming event.

I stopped on a promontory above the stream from which I could see the opposite bank and the entire flat.

The buck climbed to an open bench, crossed it, and started up the last steep bank that would put him on the flat with the herd. He topped the rise in full view of the larger rival buck, and walked directly toward the thickest concentration of does. The does and fawns didn't even glance up, but the herd buck immediately snorted a warning and came at a smooth, ground-eating run, straight as a taut string, toward the challenger.

My buck stopped, spread his legs, and lowered his head to meet the oncoming horns. Crack! The hit started a whirling spin and a rising cloud of dust. The fight, though brief, was furious. Three times around. And then they were running toward me, the challenger in the lead. With bellies to the ground and legs a blur, they sped over the grassy plain. My buck zigzagged, but it was as if his pursuer were fastened to him. The big buck came charging on, horns cocked forward, just inches behind a very vulnerable rump.

My buck got to the riverbank first and flew out into space to land on the bench below. The champion/herdmaster slued to a dusty halt at the brink and immediately trotted back to his harem, prancing a bit and ready to take on *any* buck foolish enough to challenge him.

It didn't end there. My buck, hidden below the bank, stood for a while looking up at the crest. He had lost, and he wasn't foolish enough to try another encounter. Yet — *nobody* deserves the company of that many does! The unfairness of it. What to do?

An idea came. The buck trotted downstream on the bench a hundred yards or so, then angled up the bank. But before he reached the crest, he slowed to a very careful last few steps, then stopped. Inches below the rim, he stretched his neck up cautiously until one eye could peek out at the herd through the grasses along the edge. Almost immediately he lowered his head and returned to the bench. Obviously, he could see the stronger buck and was not going to show himself.

Then he trotted quite a distance upstream and peeked again. No dice. Once more he dropped to the bench and trotted downriver so far that I had to take out my pocket glasses to watch him. Again he climbed and inched an eye up just over the rim. But this time his neck stretched higher. He turned his head so both eyes could study the flat. He took one step up. Another step, and another. Now he was up on the flat and starting toward the nearest does, not the confident warrior of the earlier challenge, but a defeated and embarrassed would-be herdmaster trying to recoup some ego and to have a harem, no matter how small, of his own. He wasn't at all sure he could pull it off, but he had to try.

The bigger buck was across the herd, screened by the many grazing does and fawns. The challenger looked as if he wanted to hide, right out there in the open. Head down, walking slowly, he tried to assume doe-like anonymity and move into the herd without disturbance. How he hoped to cut out two or three does without a major fuss once he got there was probably farther ahead than he had planned.

As it turned out, his strategy fizzled right at the start. A crack must have opened in the screening herd because a very angry, grunting, coughing big buck was coming — fast.

My buck flipped over the rim, and it was all over. At least to my eyes; the sun was sliding behind Electric Peak, and I wanted to get up into the interior of the Park for the night, to be ready for a frosty morning with bugling elk.

# FOR EVERY WINNER

After the pronghorn affair, I hiked back to my camper, The Wild Goose, put on a heavy wool sweater to ward off the quick chill that comes at sundown in the mountains, and went grinding up the long climb through the Golden Gate. It had been a month since I had arrived in Yellowstone Park to photograph wildlife. Fall weather had been delightful: two well-spaced snowstorms followed by perfect Indian summer; balmy blue days and clear frosty nights. In such weather the rut, or mating season, had come on slowly (and so had my photography). But the nights had gradually, though almost imperceptibly, become colder; and the most active time of the rut had at last arrived. Each morning and evening bull elk were bugling their exciting challenge until the mountains rang with their calls.

Once through the Golden Gate and over Kingman Pass — the northern pass through the rim of mountains that surround the high interior of Yellowstone, I could float along in high gear. I was again in sunlight as I cruised past Swan Lake.

Then I saw them, off to my right front. Eight cow elk were lined up shoulder to shoulder, and two magnificent six-point bulls were parading in front of them, stiff-legged and very deliberate. I glanced ahead and in my mirrors. No traffic either way. There was a small pull-off on the left so I coasted in and turned the key.

I slid quietly to the ground and left the door ajar so the latch wouldn't snap. I eased around the back of the truck just in time to see one of the big bulls raise his head so that his great antlers almost touched his back. He let out a long, screaming bugle that ended with three powerful bass grunts, EEEEEEEEEUNK! EUNK! YUNK!

The rival bull tore through the sage, driving twelve ivory spears into the ground and shrubs, coming up festooned like a Christmas tree until he shook his broad rack and sent the debris flying.

The elk were in deep shade at the edge of a lodgepole pine forest.

112

No chance for pictures. Besides, it was going to happen *now*. I hurried across the road and up onto a knoll, unnoticed by the animals as the tension built. I had just focused my binoculars on the bulls when they crashed together in a powerful confrontation. I analyzed the sound right then. I've heard enough antlers *clack* to know that this sound was far beyond that. The whole network of tines and beams met at once as the half-ton beasts collided.

How the antlers stood that initial impact I'll never know. Then, it was as if they were glued together. Around and around they went — first one way, then the other, and even in the cold October shade, clouds of dust were flying. Each bull kept trying to push the other off balance, hoping for a stumble and an opening to thrust those spears into the other's flesh. Yet each had to ward off the other's points with his own. I glanced at my watch as the fight progressed; it was 6:10. In the background I saw the disinterested cows running, single file, into the timber.

One bull gained a little. I could see that the other back-pedaled more than he moved forward. The fight meandered, without plan or regard for advantage, up over knolls and down into hollows. When the stronger one gained a bit, his legs churned as he pushed with low-to-the-ground power and frightening speed.

But though the weaker bull was forced back over the rough terrain maybe a hundred feet in a few seconds, he never once lost poise or balance; and when he had the advantage of a slope, he even shoved the stronger animal back a few steps.

Once there was a break in contact during some fast movement over rough ground, and I thought, "Here it comes!" But the weaker bull spun in the air, and his tines were all aimed at his opponent when the thrust came. They were apart only a second or two.

Twice more, there was a release of antlers, but each time they were realigned in time, and the could-be-fatal jab was against antlers, not flesh.

Minute after minute of this marvelous spectacle went by with practically no sound. The immense quiet intensified the drama of the event. There was only the breaking of sage when the fight moved, the crash of antlers after a brief separation, and the occasional clack as antlers changed position. But mostly there was silence.

Then late in the fight, after over ten minutes of the most intense expenditure of energy, I could hear their breathing — heavy, labored, and slow. Only an all-out mating battle could call forth the total effort that these straining animals were giving. A magnificent show — almost without an audience!

There was less spinning as the fight wore on, and more straight pushing, but even then there was an occasional jerk upward, an effort to clear the way for that one decisive thrust.

Gradually, as energy drained from the huge bodies, the fight stabilized in a hollow. I could see their backs and their antlers. Around and around they still went, back and forth, but slower now, and with only the sound of breathing. The soft ground was pulverized and silent, and the antlers were held together with a more steady, if weaker, pressure.

Then it was over. The loser came out of the hollow toward me. The winner moved unerringly toward his hard-won harem. The loser didn't come far. He flopped down in the first opening in the sage he came to. Again, I looked at my watch; 6:25. Fifteen indelible minutes. I was suddenly aware of cold fingers. I had been holding my glasses with one hand and shielding them from the bright western sky with the other. Luckily, I had put on the heavy sweater against the evening chill.

For five minutes the exhausted knight lay there. I could see his great antlers backlighted with pink, above the sage. They moved back and forth as he slowly regained his breath, his strength, and his composure. Then he stood up and looked at me, seeing me for the first time. There we stood, I admiring the majesty of this grand loser, he wondering who I was and what I was doing there.

I thought, how fine that this contest had taken place; that these great beasts had decided, in the only way possible, which of them would pass his greater strength on to the elk of the future so that they would be strong to withstand the snows and cold of winter and to perpetuate a very handsome species.

# GALLERY IV

Evaporation, condensation and gravity, taken out of the physics lab, look like *this*. Hooray!

*Mt. Rainier, Washington*

I'm thankful that the world turns . . .
*Sunrise, Black Hills, South Dakota*

. . . and that I can see.
*September, Grand Teton National Park, Wyoming*

The Yellowstone Park pronghorn buck was about forty feet
from me, broadside, but looking away.

In April I was here alone.
*Bridal Veil Falls, Yosemite National Park*

Every kind of life is unique, and it is these differences that
make living on earth the grand adventure that it is.
*Beaver dam and lodge, Grand Teton National Park,*
Wyoming

This Hayden Valley bison bull showed some interest in me,
and at this moment he had my attention, too!
*Yellowstone National Park, Wyoming*

*Mt. Rainier National Park, Washington, in October*
*(Overleaf)*

With telescopic vision and ability to move with ease on
nearby cliffs where predators cannot follow, bighorn rams
enjoy the luxury of seldom-disturbed cud-chewing.
*Yellowstone National Park, Wyoming, in February*

The stratified layers in the Grand Canyon are clearly marked pages in a geological history book going back to beyond the first life on earth. Awesome in size and grandeur, the Canyon has been an impassable barrier long enough for tassel-eared squirrels on opposite rims to develop strikingly different coloration in their tails and bellies, even though they are separated by just a few miles in some places.

Yes, it's the longest arch. But statistics are unimportant
compared to the drama, the grace, the beauty of stone,
trees, and sky.

*Landscape Arch, Arches National Park, Utah*

This young Rocky Mountain bull elk doesn't have much of
a rack this year, but *next* fall he'll be bugling with the best
of them, challenging any bull within hearing — at least until
he sees the other bull.

If you have a weak heart, don't watch bighorn mountain sheep lambs. Born on almost inaccessible ledges, they follow their mothers from one scary cliff to another to avoid predators.

Tundra growth, though low and often miniature representatives of plant life farther south, is robust and bright, *wanting* to survive, to flower, to fruit, and to reproduce on the few inches of soil warm enough to support life in brief summers.

*Low bush cranberries, Alaska, August*